P9-AFW-401

LEAVING

PHOENIX **POETS**

LATON CARTER

LEAVING

THE UNIVERSITY OF CHICAGO PRESS
Chicago and London

LATON CARTER lives in Eugene, Oregon. His work
has appeared in magazines such as *Chicago Review* and
Ploughshares.

The University of Chicago Press, Chicago 60637
The University of Chicago Press, Ltd., London
© 2004 by The University of Chicago
All rights reserved. Published 2004
Printed in the United States of America

13 12 11 10 09 08 07 06 05 04   1 2 3 4 5

ISBN: 0-226-09518-5 (cloth)
ISBN: 0-226-09519-3 (paper)

Library of Congress Cataloging-in-Publication Data

Carter, Laton.
   Leaving / Laton Carter.
      p.   cm.—(Phoenix poets)
   ISBN 0-226-09518-5 (cloth : alk. paper)
   ISBN 0-226-09519-3 (pbk. : alk. paper)
   I. Title.

   PS3603.A7775L43 2004
   811'.6—dc22

                                        2004000651

This book is for Kirk.

There is still time—in the lee, in the quiet, in the extraodinary light.

— ROBERT ADAMS

Contents

Acknowledgments

Grateful acknowledgment is made to the periodicals in which these poems first appeared:

Alaska Quarterly Review: "Indication"
Notre Dame Review (no.9, Winter 2000): "Scarce," "Decision"

LEAVING

Oblique

A girl leans down to her bicycle's handlebars.
The light changes, her right foot pushes against its pedal.
Something makes her mouth half-smile. Then, as if to check this,
no, she shakes her head.

Contained in her idle car, a woman hears
mostly air-conditioning. In the turn lane,
too far back to make this light, she forgets to advance — her own skin was
paler, but hair long like that, for fingers and worry.

He's waking up. Down the off-ramp, the bus slows, hesitates, at the light
pulls to a stop. Now he'll count cats with Barbara. Yesterday was their record:
nine. She's in the seat behind him and others are quiet or asleep when she says
four, five, he adds *six*. And her voice again: *A new one, seven — a kitten*.

The city darkens, is illuminated. To the passenger, from such altitude,
its parts move unfastened, through each other.

Diurnal

Winter mornings with low clouds,
dashboard lights reflecting against each driver,
anyone overtaking another can see into that
second space. One driver, with her free hand,

picks the skin at either side where her lips meet.
Another, his focus shifting from the mirror to the road and back again,
aligns then pats down the hair across his head. Another, it's the wrist,
the underside: stainless steel and glass, how late or early.

An expressway means drivers can move their cars
faster. As it left- or right-exits, it
remains express and adds sidewalk. On a day off or
not yet to work, a woman walks her dog:

a patch of crabgrass, the dog's nose, the volume of air
separating her body from the dog's, the leash penetrating this volume,
engine sound encapsulating it, city blocks
stretching it, having it give way to on-ramps and overpasses.

A cubicle is a box with the top cut off, one side
fully or partially removed. A worker doesn't look at
another worker, rather plastic veneer or pixels. Inside one,
a child's tempera finger painting is

pinned to the nonflammable fabric wall.
Outside the double-paned windows of office buildings, behind
tinted windows of a bus, a commuter
brushes against his nostrils the soft hair of his forearm:

chlorine. Hours ago, another city, the
brilliant pool that suspended his body.

Brief Hesitation

A woman wakes at five.
Because the one rule of the commuter van
is no talking once the vehicle reaches the highway,

she's free to sleep or follow the discontinuous mix
of phrases and voices that play in her thinking,
see them fit or not fit with the landmarks and signposts
she watches from the passenger window.

Rain droplets scurry horizontally against the glass;
she doesn't sleep.

A work day is a single, complete execution
of periodically finished and unfinished tasks.
On either side of work, before it and after it in one day,
all the same objects within sight and available to be cared about.

What knowledge a person does or does not have
of any one same object is its taking hold.

Because it is able to be seen into or
only at its surface, an object is assigned meaning.
Vague, wandering meaning
apprehends a viewer as much as what is physically painful, poignant.
Taken hold of, a viewer longs to witness again her own repetition:

at 6:20, backed-up cars of factory workers at Exit 199;
the billboard just north of Albany and the pulp mills, its LED display showing
what number of million dollars the interstate lottery holds;
past Scio, mint compost at $6.00 per cubic yard.

      To care is
almost to be doing something.
She likes cauliflower, blue cheese dressing, Saltines.

Eating lunch, she can go over what she wants to
do, have that be her own,
the very difference that helps her keep facing each next work day,

the drive with its chain of objects, the chain in reverse,
her shoes at last off and left in the kitchen.

Continuous

Across a synapse, a signal
passes away from a nerve cell to its
target tissue. Fingers

repeat their motion, strike down or
keep their same arched posture enough so that tendons
inflame, compress the median nerve within the carpus.

Proper to a body is its own pain, each
particular discomfort more or less noticeable between cumulative
use or rest. Taking

hers to a grocery store, a woman buys
oranges, sourdough bread and margarine, watches them
leave her hand on the register's carousel.

In line and to her left, from the blue veins of his forearm to the
biceps to the shirt's sleeve and shoulder, there is a neck, an
unshaven chin. Her focus

shifts behind him to what her peripheral vision
tells her is another's focus: a woman's,
already fixed on her, meaning possession and *no*.

Before sunrise, a city uses
artificial light to see and be seen. In white halogen
or incandescent yellow, unfocused by winter fog,

all the day's initial goings-on
appear in miniature. Driving, a man numbers on each block every
one person outside and moving.

The world is not scenery to
anyone who has work to do in it. The man has
favorite trees. Knowing they will

be there when his car meets that one point on the
highway's horizon, they help him remember that
what he has his body do is forgettable.

As part of a city,
a river opens itself
less as an object of inspection than

something to be trained. Impossible
to train his focus on any one portion's movement, the man
understands of the river human reaction: government or fear.

After it has been kept six weeks in
cold and darkness, a hyacinth can be forced. January,
dead grass and half-frozen mud outside, the bulb

inside will send forth its narrow green leaves, the
funnel-like corolla. Because it is unnatural, the practice requires
help of one's body to be accomplished.

Outside of what one can do for oneself,
two is necessary for help to happen. Unhelped,
the body longs for another, makes whole

the number between longing and help. To change,
in the optative sense, is to be static: *If*, repeated,
equals one, makes one's company one's own longing.

Though not grown for harvest, a winter cover crop
reduces erosion, helps improve soil tilth. Before
significant rainfall or the first frost, a farmer can seed

alfalfa, yellow-blossom sweetclover, hairy vetch. Come spring,
the crop should be incorporated as green manure or
killed and left as no-till mulch, ready for summer's grids and traffic.

Counter

He writes *6 a.m.*, *7 a.m.*, down to noon,
and starts again with numbers,
all with spaces in between for the half-hour.

If, at 6, he feeds the cats, follows the template he's
tried to leave as open as possible,
he can feel better about what he is or isn't doing.

Joblessness means needing to find worth in
anything that's not money.
Transfixed at the kitchen sink, he peels an orange, studies the drain.

Everywhere, other jobs were being worked,
each worker, in degrees, more or less present
to whatever task made up their compensation.

A bird outside the window, his own breathing, and
again he's caught himself: his body in abeyance to time.
Guilty, self-reproaching, he returns two books he bought yesterday.

The body needs its own use that thinking doesn't want.
Blood is in his stool again. The brace,
meant to support the lower back while sitting,

has put pressure on the colon.
The chair, with its pillows, creates a reverse pressure,
dilating the veins in now swollen anal tissue.

He should stand up, stretch, be anything but static.
At the park, in the sun,
parents kick a soccer ball or push the merry-go-round for their children.

The day is Saturday.
Because he's with no one other person, he's that much conscious of his
wanting invisibility, or to at least stop and watch.

One girl, too old to not be embarrassed by parents,
sits in the shade. She watches her responsibility, two boys,
wrestle in the grass, her bored face glossy with acne.

      A grocery store is a last place.
Each with a separate list and thought, a person must walk aisles,
wait as others wait, distracted or alert, in channels curved around each register.

Recounting the number in his basket,
he's standing in front of the yogurt section when he notices her,
maybe too close, maybe waiting for him to move.

In its timidness, her smile means she's patient or safe.
To hold her gaze any longer than necessary to communicate the same
would make too public his attachment to people.

Properly averting his focus and turning,
he walks somewhere else, anywhere, a half-smile still across his face.

Silence

There is an unmeasured distance between two people that means,
if they do not already know each other, they do not have to talk.

The distance narrowed, the two points moving toward each other,
causes decision: what necessary act of salutation or aloofness.

Glass dividing this distance obviates the act.
Behind a windshield or double-pane storm window,

a person's separation allows for closer, less regulated study of the other.

To watch and comprehend with implicit understanding another person's
movements as either reminiscent of or foreign to what one knows,

one is easily taken to another part of one's thinking:
any fragment of memory, a suggestion of a familiar person.

The kinesics of the face, watched unmonitored from a distance,
issues its own private speech. When the distance is at once collapsed,

the face's eyes drawing a line to the watcher's eyes, the speech too collapses.

Tentative

The plastic lip of the laundry basket,
where it fits against her hip, has split open.
It pinches up the hem of her shirt.

In the middle of the work,
between the bedroom closet and the washer in the garage,
the voice of her friend: how she might say it,
how her bravado is both affected and comforting.

If you don't want to, then don't.
Even though she doesn't have children, something
immediate and weighing on her decisions, the idea seems
too easy, self-contented.

Instead, her body feels pulled,
drawn by some other power, obligation or money,
incrementally away from what might be important.

Just having someone's fingers touch her head.
She doesn't need her hair cut, but wants that closeness:
warm water, massaging circles, the smell of shampoo.

The mall, despite its people, seems lifeless, too bright.
Just outside, the parking lot's asphalt is rich with the day's heat.

When she lets it, her thinking moves cinematically:
narrow, fleecy bands of cirrus give way to the lazy flight of a crow,
its view, grid of yellow paint and lampposts,
heads emerging from and disappearing under car tops.

The engine is idling. Somebody walks past.
She pretends she's looking for something.

Driving the overpass, the possibilities of what next:
telephone someone, anticipate her own voice against the mouthpiece,
is it hers, what ease is there.

A thought can be stepped back from,
watched from a close remove. As it accumulates meaning,
the necessity of words grows unwieldy, breaks off.

To remember a thought, she plays in reverse
each edit. Like a conversation that moved freely and without mark,
how did I get here is uncovered by tracing a string of refractions,
one idea that bent into another.

Inside, she turns on the fans, changes her shirt.
Opening the closet door, she's forgotten about the laundry basket.
Where it usually rests, a blank space of hardwood, dust.

She looks at her arm, the shirt in her hand. What's happened of the day
plays itself back, parts count or don't, how many should count,
could anything change. With her free hand, she half-shuts the door,
meets her face in the long mirror, her hair almost dry.

With

He's laughing so hard he's bent over. His friend,
stuck under bags of groceries and in the crib of the cart, rolls
backward from the sidewalk toward the intersection. Cars

pause. He doesn't move, maybe he
can't, and his friend has traveled into the street, his mouth now
too uncontrollably open.

10 p.m. She knows her hair smells of
vegetable shortening, hamburgers. She's walked that
one small space since before noon, minus

one half-hour and two ten-minutes. Clocked out,
the last thing is the garbage. From the dumpster, her car,
air she wants kept on her face.

The street she drives automatically, passengerless
and mute. At the intersection, she thinks only of the shower.

Interval

The rain has stopped.
In the yellow half-light of late afternoon,
starlings huddle in the courtyard,
peck the bruised meat of fallen apples.

Again,
I have lost my job.
The man on the telephone explains I have
used up my unemployment compensation.

Everything is uncomfortable:
the silence of the house, the drowsy
unbemused face of the cat,
the muscles around my mouth.

Now the starlings are gone
I cannot avoid myself.

Yield

Outside of Amity, but not outside the city limits,
there is, for 100 yards, a 40 miles per hour speed zone.
An officer positions his automobile at 1st and Trade streets under
the shade of a fir tree. He knows

the statute number by memory: 811.100.
My uncle says bail is the city's revenue; most checks support
the four schools or the fire department; the same's
also true for Monmouth, Sherwood.

Because of its size and the satisfaction of knowing there'll be only
one clerk, it's Yeager's I walk to
to buy milk. A quart is near double the cost than at the supermarket.
I like the two small formica-topped tables, the men in

jeans and flannel shirts who sit there eating
65¢ bear claws as they pencil in numbers on lottery forms they
don't buy. I tell myself it's more than a place to postpone the
deciding of what's next. Away from them on 11th, my

own postponing advances, hesitates.
Houses are a way of seeing one's self out of one's body. I can
displace my walking: sitting at the window of the 10th and Taylor house, I'm
up one floor at the dormer, blue hydrangeas below. It doesn't last:

me sitting at the window would notice me walking; I'm placed
back into my body and me. When I say or think it, *home*
doesn't register as a house I could walk past, but where
already I'm inside: the uncomfortable sofa, yesterday's Help Wanted.

Berg's Ski Shop has an air pump. Outside, out of a hole in the west wall's
brick and mortar, cracked and sprawling, the tubing's faded black is
crowned by the pitted steel of the AMFLO 100 gauge.
No coins: bicyclists dismount, press

one thumb on a tire, the other the trigger. The sound
of pressurized oxygen in clipped bursts reaches the brown apartments on
13th and Lawrence where, still in uniform, a waiter
stops to check the mailbox before taking the staircase to his room.

Sleep

The cats have made no money.
On the towel she left to sop up
dishwater from the kitchen tile,
the black one has fit himself.

I sit on the lawn chair; the smell of warm earth
mixes with apples, a barbecue somewhere. The neighbor's son
wants to be a helicopter. Too tired to pick him up,
I let him drape his body over my legs.

Small life: my uncle had shown me the star,
two stars that were an eye exam. Discernible,
proper to themselves, one picked them out, was contented.
Firmament offered us back to ourselves.

This once, eloquence is useless —
no need to praise.

Render

Why you won't shop at the grocery store on 11th
is why I do: how the people there
talk and act. Their stories and jobs,
the corresponding assumptions we make
interest me less than the very disclosure
that's there to witness: a son
pleading with his mother over a kind of cereal,
a man deliberating over prices and quantity of meat.

Though it's healed, I'm trained
to alert to your tendonitis. A can
of black beans, your box of shirts from the attic —
I think the isolated cold you describe;
how, as if it might find release out of the
tips of your fingers, you thrashed then massaged your hands.
Mostly, though, the failure in your voice, your
pink brush dropped and left on the bathroom floor.

The differences between us are what I say and
resay when you're asleep and I'm
quiet with my eyes open in the dark room.
Though it can't be resaid, my half of
any one conversation we've had is what I correct
before I sleep. It's your appetite for
seeing things done that fastens my wanting you and
also makes heavier my shyness in accepting that I can

stare at any stupid object in the house for hours and
never have it be what I'm thinking.

I'm tired of arguing.
I bought the mango because it seemed a thing
so unlike what either of us would think of that,
perhaps, we'd be surprised into a new way of talking.
You'd already been practicing. In the trash on
folded sheets of your stationery: *You give me*
encouragement, but it's not unconditional —
I know I don't think as much as you and I
shouldn't feel guilty but I do —
What is it you see in me?

The Geese

When it happened, I was in bed. Even though there was
nothing to see, I opened my eyes, stared into darkness.
Outside, far above, they were navigating the black sky.
I just lay there, listening.

Each call separate but part of one
succession of calls. One sheet of sound.
I swear I could hear their wings beat,
displacing each moment, troubling the cold air.

Now they've gone, there are no days.
The geese took them. All that's left is rain. Wet
asphalt and muddied grass. The next morning
there was no morning and the geese were gone.

Their flight was passage once,
now unchangeable leaving.

Away

I wonder if the VCR will work, the old movies you'd
said you'd wanted to see. The place, when I got in,
was littered with bodies of ants. Before unloading the car,
I vacuumed — you would have shook your head, laughed.

I can recall your face precisely, easily, maybe for the first time, and not
mix it as I usually do, as I've done with others, with that
first face. My guilt extends itself, is honest:
it's true I say your name aloud mostly when I'm angry.

You'll make jam, forget to change the cat's water,
I won't close the blinds. At the end of the day, have I done
anything, does thinking count, I haven't rubbed your arms.

I lie awake in the dark, afraid of my old job,
afraid of no job. Your leg touching mine would be
not consolation but good distraction, letting me exhale.

Sequence

On the counter, one plate, just so. To the right, a fork, a spoon:
parallel lines with enough space in between.
The tumbler and mug are hand dried, each placed
mouth up. The sponge, wrung dry, rests near the faucet.

Salt is in the fog passing over the house.
He is embarrassed for wanting to attach meaning.

The hope in order
is assurance. That an object, person, or idea can be
left, be unchanged when returned to, is
order's promise.

The promise of salt is to preserve,
decay, is a promise of violence:
meat pickles, the car's muffler is rusting.

Out of his control, the kitchen window films over.
To force sympathy between what he sees and thinks,
to create metaphor, is playful want, lazy.
Open to damage, tender,

care is what's left.
He can care about something actual, let it mean
only he is affected by the world:

a girl who stops her play on the sidewalk, as he passes
offers her small voice in greeting;
a collarless tabby who, when he crouches down,
bumps and brushes against his knees.

The increase of disorder
distinguishes the past from the future, giving
direction to time. In time,
he will go back again to that changed person:

the one who has let him go, the one who will
again welcome him; whose modest smile
attests to and admits the difficulty and care between them.

Momentum

So many thoughts this morning, between Jackson and Polk: three blocks.
If I look hard enough, at my shoes or the concrete, I can see nothing,
slowly draw up distant parts of myself, whatever is beyond my standard guilt.

I need to find a better job, I need to save money, I need to be efficient with time
is suspended as long as I keep my body in its same movement.

The dog surprises me. I don't care about my pants or its muddied paws,
but it doesn't have a tag, won't stop wanting to follow me.
Before I can get onto Almaden, it's brought back the pinecone.

Do I have a place?
Trained somehow to measure worth in whatever can be seen,
I can't see where I might fit. If I did have a place,
how would it rest with me, would I yield or rise to it?

No one is out, not even in cars. The dog hears something, bounds off.
Even alone, I feign a disregard for self-consciousness.
When I stop to study the magnolia, I want
only to be a person engaged in one thing.

Instead, I am also whoever might just have woken up,
who, while looking out the kitchen window, draws water into the tea kettle,
notices this person stopped in front of their house, thinks this or that.

The magnolia is nothing.
I am the compulsion of scrutiny:

again, discovering and crossing out the idea of value,
of how to belong, of too many separate histories.
Trying at once to embrace everything overwhelming,
there's still room for the local: the pulse in my legs, cut grass, an animal.

Ever

Because she's thinking of money,
she forgets the twenty dollar bill in her hand.
The quick-stop mart is air-conditioned,
a man has said something.

The remainder of one subtraction
is added to by interest.
How much of a subtraction she'll make, mail out,
she computes pushing open the glass door into gasoline vapor.

A moment can sustain in the memory
not for what it represents visually
but as a cause of thought attached to it.

If the thought, timely and local,
dissolves in the mix of newer thoughts, is eventually
forgotten, only the external representation remains:

keys in her left hand, a pant leg;
on the other side of the car and above its roof,
before their eyes might meet, the tanned face of the attendant.

Bruxism is involuntary,
habitual. The point of compression is noticed
always after: a sleeper wakes, is chastened by throb.

She can steer with her left hand. The right,
trained enough so that she can attend to something else,
massages just under the ear at the jaw.

The day's light is hard, just overhead.
Certain windshields of opposing traffic,
when they reach that same angle, turn white,
click off as immediately as they came on.

The brain registers too much.
Before the vague attending nausea, descriptions one would make
in the company of a doctor or friend, like a sign, pass through her thinking.

She can get home.
If she can get home, she can undo it.
With however much dark and stillness, she can return to herself,
will another making of her person.

      The water glass she left out sweats;
the cubes of ice have shrunken into hardened pearls.
So many hours of the day, a day off, feel wasted.

Outside the quiet of her apartment, the neighbor's son has his plastic figurines,
floating in his hands in the air, talk to each other.
To her, from behind the window, their world is mute. Only their bodies,
stiff and bouncing, signify dialogue.

No one is talking.
To avoid replaying all the day's small but cumulative frustrations,
she has to catch herself. The half-conscious trance at the window,
comfortable at first, will let her worrying seep back in.

The honeydew is cold, awakening against her palate.
Plastic container, fork; standing in shirt and boxers —
that she moved from the boy to the kitchen seems not to have happened.

She looks down at her feet:
bare, artless couple. Their deference makes her smile.
She has the toes splay, huddle.

The body, released from pain,
begins again. She won't watch television.
So much hostility and irrelevance wants more than gives.

She wants to give.
When she thinks of giving,
she can stand back from her life.

What concerns her,
the timely payment of any one bill, what she's accomplished in what time,
can be forgettable, fade.

Now
plus now. Sometimes she feels infinite.
Composed only of caring, her ability to give
might rework in her a way to see:

before the calendar's next day,
the expanse of the evening; the blinding convention
of compensation forestalled, translated
into a calling, a devotion.

Twilight

On the back step, I hear your voice from inside.
In order to know where you might be, with the pressure on my ears,
the loss of accuracy and distinction, I try to gauge
the time it takes from the bathroom, the hall closet.

The weather has been so much heat then rain,
and I have gotten better and worse. Days mean
nothing regular, only what stretches, pulls.

What must this be like for you.
In the self-absorption of understanding illness,
I have only listened in exhaustion, seen you
watch me fight sleep.

You come to the door, toothbrush in mouth,
and, at once, it is right to suspend my usual refusal of sentiment:
Darling, I say, and I let myself say it again.

Finding One's Way

Generated by molten iron
moving inside its core,
the Earth's geomagnetic field

marks itself in three:
a north pole and south, an equator.

Field lines sprout
at ninety-degree angles

away from a magnetic pole,
curve back toward Earth to reach its equator where,

at once horizontal to the planet's surface, and without resting,
they are drawn to the opposing magnetic pole.

A semicircle formed, the lines finish
their unfinishable performance: a circle,
infinite circles.

In the clover fields of southeastern Canada,
a bobolink breaks through its shell.

Alive, already into a separate life,
it can't yet understand, doesn't need
yet to understand

inclination angles, magnetoreception,
what, before autumn and its first frost, will have
already been mastered.

Better now to feed and be fed,
rest under the care and trust of protection, while

just beneath the dermis and delicate skull,
microscopic and lodged in certain brain cells,

iron oxide crystals register the Earth's applied torque,
directing a way.

Of migrant songbirds in the Americas,
the bobolink's course is the longest and most dangerous.

For sometimes more than six-thousand miles
until it finds suitable grasslands in Argentina,
the adolescent and adult together

navigate by environmental and geomagnetic cues.

With no lodestar on overcast nights,
their ferromagnetic compass directs them toward the equator.
Before crossing the Caribbean Sea,

it molts and feeds in coastal marshland,
earns the slang *Reed Bird*, *Rice Bird*, and,
after landfall in Jamaica, its metabolism slowed, *Butter Bird*.

The Atlantic is what's left,
horizon with no land, the unpredictability of weather.

A person need only predict so much.
Possessing the molecular apparatus to do it,
but lacking internal imperative,

migration for a human is dispensable.

Preadjusted so that her time can be her own,
she gives it up for the social framework
of buying it back.

After work, the joint imperative of a society,
she is exhausted.

What's unsatisfied in her as she sits at the kitchen table opening mail
is a question not of more power to buy

but of a way, a one way

buried under so many contingencies
there never was one way.

On top of the parking structure
where a woman she read about in the newspaper
forsook one morning her shaken bearing,

her car's engine ticks time against a cool wind.
In the time it will take to close the distance
between her body and her body working —

the elevator, crosswalk, employee entrance, time card —
the ticks will slow inversely to what must have sped up:

the woman's heart, any last inarticulable thought.

Not nothing,
the suicide was a way
into nothing.

She can't think too long on it, time
anyway requires otherwise.

    The more time requires her attention,
the easier it elapses.

White bar towels in diluted bleach water,
any forgettable number of tables, the same
one shy face of the regular who wants to flirt:

the mosaic of a day
won't let itself be forced into a sum,
anything that might add up to more than a simple

rearranging of its parts.

To her body in its thought and movement,
change feels impossible,
is what she wants most.

In bed, before the next day, the permissible
honest change of her touch against herself.

    The rows of the nursery suggest order.
Sedum and fern, black plastic trays of succulent ground cover
suspend in droplets the morning's watering.

He sighs.
The physical distance from home, a handful of miles away,
only makes larger his procrastination.

Enough surface area
for no less than four of the moss's
miniature pink blossoms to fit on his smallest fingernail,

his looking at his own hand
translates into what will happen shortly —

his hand on the steering wheel, the closing up of obligation —

as now, as it could only appear to anyone else,
his hand is singular, testing the plant's spongy weight.

  The two-ness of thought is that,
in thinking, the world is replaced
by another, imagined world.

The road, especially as he's driven it before,
is less a road. Instead, he sees his daughter:
should he have said that, how might it now be corrected,

how much will she listen.

For a human, automation frees up
attention to being. Not having to be,
he can riddle over playing and replaying the past.

With freight of so many possible negatives,
his worrying substitutes what's actual —

not driving, but what trouble, can he erase it,
is it already unavoidably permanent.

Responsibility necessitates a tending
to more than one. One's way becomes

one's two ways,
person two autonomous enough, but under the care of person one.
Her bike is still in the garage, the time for the bus

still future.
No music on, but she's there in her room, and,
he can't help it, he's apologizing,

not explaining as he'd promised himself.

Wanting maybe too strongly to be forgiven or loved
in the unconditional way he's reserved for her,
if she would look up it could mean that return,

he pauses for it, her gaze on him in almost any way,
now, here, the air between them charged.

Getting Lost

The bus means she doesn't have to think.
If she could, or if it never stopped,
she'd ride it forever.

As cargo, one can be heedless,
dumb to knowing.
Unaltered as the next landscape is penetrated,

she's practically invisible,
as she'd have it.

Through her filmy partial reflection,
other problems, there on sidewalks and at traffic lights,

not hers to have to possess.

For the time it will take the driver to complete the circuit,
she can sink into the detached coziness
of lulled, half-mindful observation.

The trick is her God.
Aloof, fallible, sometimes lazy,
ordinary and lovable,

God was hers.
Her own, not the ever-burdened,
unbelievably perfect one mandating subscriptions elsewhere.

Someone intentionally evasive but romantic,
God would leave signs, God
kept you interested enough.

Why is this happening to me? wasn't a question that got asked,
nor *This is God's Way* a faith abided.

Insulation to the world,
God was a reliable entanglement, a private
substitute for everyone not listening.

  East, away from the ocean,
past everything she can see and because maps said so,
desert.

No people.
Or, people who kept quiet, scratching notes in journals
because of the desert:

-ologists of some kind,
their job was to attend, to study.

Now if her atoms could disconnect,
the flesh across her body painlessly dissipate,
be absorbed into and transport through the bus's wall,

in one hot wind carry to that white
concentrated line that was the horizon,
sure home of never having to mean.

The body of water does not say it is.
Rock-bound, delivered from a deep
subterranean aquifer through a geological fault,

it only is.

Being is, its place apart from other
larger or smaller bodies, from what the desert had once been,
doesn't need to count.

Virtually uncountable,
the time it took for glacial evaporation,
the mountain range to ascend high enough

so that coastal precipitation got blocked,
the land eastward eventually denied moisture,
counted only as change.

Time as change already was, had already been being is.

From the alkaline soil,
saltbush, creosote. To the hole in the earth,
its flooded cave system and algae,

post-Pleistocene isn't long gone.

The sides of the limestone chamber just now
touched again by rising water that fell to the earth's surface
thousands of years earlier,

light can only plumb so far.
In less murky water, and within the shallow confine
of one 13-foot shelf,

the pupfish spawns.

Having been closely followed by her consort
until the last egg was deposited,
it's now time to rest.

At just under one inch,
the Devil's Hole pupfish checks
time's mutability.

Unchanged for nearly thirty-thousand millennia,
its genetic code suggests a continuum
that holds still.

Into itself, and with no carryings from one place to another,
the code can't claim part to anything exactly beyond the one self.

Time waits,
the pupfish is the same and lost,
preserved, but with nothing present to belong.

Almost outside it, its time
is space, the very physical texture and arrangement of what gets sensed,
an indefinite suspension of the possible, the is.

Too much in asking to wait.
The bed of the truck is already loaded,
a tarp pulled over its contents.

In the wind, the top boughs of the big leaf maple
sway. Face down or up and in no noticeable pattern,

its leaves mottle the driveway.

Some petioles like antennae sprouted from the concrete,
they give then flatten under the tires backing out from the garage.

Headlights, wipers, before the mailbox and street and in
however long it takes to recount *Do I have everything*,
one more thing:

its five lobes outstretched, splayed as fingers
catching air, the leaf is caught,
sealed now by rainwater over polyurethane and the tire well.

      For almost four hundred miles,
I-84 East. Boise, then I-15 South for three hundred more.
Utah for eighty miles, and before Wyoming and Uinta Drive,

I-80 for one hundred and twenty more: the parts
navigable by freeway, and with patience as it comes and goes,
easy enough. There are still smaller roads,

then no road, marked and unmarked paths to be made over sod that,
after late summer rain, pulls at one's boots.

North of Green River and its trona mines,
Pinedale, the ranger station. Before the tarp is pulled back,
one quick sweep of all it's accumulated.

Someone's son notices first.
Alien, as big as his face, he picks it up at the stem.
Maybe someone will watch, it's on fire, his tongue dares a flame.

In the saliva, any number of dead skin cells are left.
Never thought about, they mix with water, air on every
available side. To them, their unarticulated difference means

they are no different than certain attached hydrogen molecules
twenty miles away at Knapsack Col.

At 12,200 feet in Wyoming's Wind River Range,
the source of the Green River, master stream of the Colorado,
yields again its share of so many million-

billion molecules internal to the earth's deeper strata.

They move now into all their chances of reaching past
1700 miles, past Fontenelle and Flaming Gorge dams early on,
four states, eight dams and a country later,

dry riverbed, mudbar shallows. Increasingly, a current,
tamarisk and great blue heron en route to El Golfo de Santa Clara.

Indication

The winter light balances with the light inside houses,
for a moment steadies, then breaks, dies again.

On my walk, people are in their kitchens.
From another room, the cold blue light of the television
flickers wildly against a woman's cheeks, her forehead.

In my mind I hear your ecstatic
postured voice. The praise you heaped this summer
on blackberries, the rolling beauty of words you couldn't
not say twice.

Life is not boundless.
As much as I loved your loving of things, I knew
we would go back. I would be the same.

In the calm regularity of streets and seconds, the space I make for worry.

Story

To hear you tell it, I know you're only sharing,
it makes me see the difference. I'm
not envying, if you'll believe that, I want good for you.

What I want is those young girls' laughter.
They bumped my knees running past and
didn't notice. Their mouths were open.

Shedding an attraction to despair is
why I continue to face people. I know
you don't think like this. My jaw aches from it.

Everything happens for a reason. Is that
a gauge of fortitude or a way to excuse it? Putting
words to suffering, in the end, is a terrible bore.

I do cry.
Always at my desk. I think
Sister. And that I'm one too.

I picture it sometimes: you in the car, laughing,
too many people, no one with their own space,
the very sound of it, so much human sound.

Scarce

Just barely. And just
like her, never overdoing, never coming out with it,
always by implication: I smelled the letter's perfume.

What if Jeanne had gone for the mail?
She'd have known faster. I had to
check and recheck to believe myself.

What's never consummated
remains enacted — I mean,
at least for her, it's never died.

Having it *dead* wouldn't make it so.
Certain moments — one particular
touch, a word with a specific inflection —

they graft themselves onto memory: what I think of
but can't mention. I was never so frightened to hear my
own name, her fingertips tracing my jaw.

Decision

I haven't known him a year. But
I know him: I'll say a word — then, whatever idea
it poses for him sends him spiraling. His voice
drops, rises. *Eager,*

I think. If he's charming, trying to be, he's good at
not showing intention. I've seen women star-eyed. But
I'm no authority — am bruised like
anyone else who follows an instinct for possessing

something vulnerable. I don't mean *some*thing,
I mean my life. And if he says it a second time —
to admit is to empower, I'll know he's
not empathetic but young.

Still, I can't lie.
When he said he smelled my hair on the pillowcase for
two days afterward, I believe him. Why
do I resent wanting?

Orion's belt, dagger at his hip;
someone practicing the clarinet; smiling, tasting
salt in the air: even then, I maintained
a voice free of trust or longing.

Between

It doesn't consume me. Or if it does, not
entirely. As much as I'd like it, I'm
not outside myself: where she sees me.

Self-consciousness, alone, protracted,
is, eventually, a form of vanity. I want seeing into things
not to dislocate me. And it's that: want.

The paper boy, half-awake or asleep, has
himself to the morning. Coincident with his work,
whatever he's thinking: cereal, his pillow, a song.

She could know. Know it's not
simple brooding, stumbling over anger, but a constant
figuring of things.

The mistakes I made into words;
attending regret; the difficulty of joy.

Separate

Everything, for him, has to be earned.
What do you want? and there was that pause.
If I gave an answer, then I'd have to,
we'd have to earn it.

It's work. And when I think that I think my job and I
hate my job. Why can't it be like
when we met? He sang; I didn't have to
say how I felt.

Not escape. I want
time — not for thinking but for
not thinking. He tugs his sideburns; it's
thought and his tic.

Of course I have dreams. When he
holds me, is silent, they surface: again and mine.

After

I stood in the doorway, looking in. Already,
the place was too quiet. I light candles daily now —
I don't think *shrine* or *memorial*. When the window is closed
their light is small and calm. I sit still and look into them.

A little girl screamed in joy and it sounded
like a seagull. My back was to her. The bird's cry
made me lose all location. I turned to see what it was.
Before I could smile or study her, she was swept up by her mother.

I haven't spoken for two days. That's not true.
I've spoken: tail ends of sentences, fragments of questions.
Sometimes it can't be my voice. This afternoon,
I stood with the refrigerator door open, looking in for nothing.

Clarity. And distraction. I wanted
the first above all; the second I refused. Your tone
went from patient to impassive. Later, you must have
reopened your book, gone back some sentences.

New Distances

I can't name them by their calls but
hazard names when I see them out the back window
on the avocado's branches. I guess

chickadee, saying the word like their song.
Mornings others I don't see
join to make a chorus. When she phones

I open the screen door and hold out the receiver.
She can't believe the volume and I say
I whistle and sometimes think I'm communicating.

Seven months and my back is bad. She can apply for
area technical trainer, regional coordinator,
in-store supervisor. I do stretches

lying on the carpet, feel the pull at my spine
where I've started wearing a brace.
For the interview she'll have to fly to Ventura.

Lately we've been mailing a box back and forth,
each time with new contents: for me, tea and soap;
for her, earrings and a children's book —

it's a change from those calls that last longest
and never resolve; that last after we've hung up.
What irreconcilability we couldn't fathom earlier

now makes sense of why I can go on about something
as unarguable as birds. Then, earlier, we didn't need the details of our faces.
We looked at other things: the stairway to my studio,

the footlocker hoisted from the trunk of my car,
my landlord's roses, my landlord in pajamas
standing as we moved from the car to the stairway,

car to the stairway, the corners of his mouth
glinting sugar crystals from doughnuts we learned
later from the carton in the trash.

Highway, Waiting

Like any other Ford, that
same American shape. Except

he can tell hers apart, the vinyl on top
chapped by heat and peeling.

He looks for this car, even if it's not coming,
staring, silent and patient, checking for its silhouette.

His eyes become good at this test,
never missing a car, skipping a roof.

He runs the image in his mind, sees it
on the highway, flaring white to red, but

real or vision, each one
not hers ticks another moment.

Turning from his lookout he walks away,
knows then: her calm passage from sight.

Shaving

Gray hair not gray but deep
brown flecked white. Beard or sideburn,
equal in length and random in pattern, they've fallen not
in the sink but round it. A frame,

inches and water spots away, houses a woman.
Foxed, unfocused except her face, monochromatic, the photo's too
old to be a lover. But intimate, this nearness of
hurried routine and stasis.

Sinks belong to days
more than desks. What's typical, the desk's photo
angled at the corner, proves
less grave, less memorable than a face at the level of

water, trimmed hair, the arrival of another morning.
This face endures, in its repetition is indelible, a reminder of what's
gone, even as he's gone without wiping up this job, eager to
get to her, the other, the lover.

Return

The linoleum tiles in the kitchen
bubble, separate. Cooking, my
heel, ball of my foot give way.

To shower, first I turn the sink on hot.
Naked, holding out my hand, the water takes
enough time that I bow, close my eyes.

December I hated mud; the city
for never filling the alley's potholes with new gravel.
Rain beat the rain in puddles.

I'm home.
Habituated to driving that I now don't have to do, but
do anyway, east out Highway 22.

Iron Mountain still has an operative ranger station.
The logbook's last two names: Lupe Wilson, Nancy Ashlock.
No one though. Beggar chipmunks, fireweed.

The neighbors' son presses his face to my screendoor, says
hi, hi, what are you doing. In Merrill, Oregon, on my way
back, I stopped, pictured myself there with work.

Two

You had to fire Eddie.
We discussed Louis Armstrong's versions of "Stardust" —
I was eating cereal, you were ironing your new work shirts.

All summer I've contended with ideas. To say *I* followed by
failed or *want* isn't false but
flat. *Deep in my* or *with all my* makes meaning top-heavy.

Everyone begins with a 90-day probation period.
Any delinquency — tardiness, failure to be in proper
uniform, repeated customer complaints — is sufficient grounds.

Scat is jazz singing in which improvised,
meaningless syllables are sung to a melody. Louis Armstrong
dropped the lead sheet. "Scat" and "jazz" have no etymologies.

Today was going to be a bad day.
The regional manager was coming in so no lunch break.
At the typewriter your wrists throb worse.

Putting on your coat you say you haven't time to think.
I rinse the bowl, unplug the iron, fold the board, and know
I do. Everything neither of us can change.

Unspoken

At noon, in the YMCA locker room,
men ignore the television, and the television is loud.
The brackets of their time require everything be simultaneous:

casual chatter, complaining, socks pulled off,
shirts and trousers hung, lacing up of court shoes.
Uncontained, their voices sink and rise.

I pull on swim trunks.
Having nothing to say, my body is my only voice.
Tall as I am, I feel slight, fragile.

The pool has its own loudness.
In my head, the world of my breathing.

At night, you notice in the courtyard raccoons,
their delicate hands; how, as if blind, they feel their way around.
Tentative, you say, and I pause.

Into

Their filigree work I dismissed as
something left out from your sewing box.
Caught again in another indeterminate morning,
vacuuming was my consolation.

Stray silver threads: their trails
vanished under the brush. Never did I see
one dried rind of a body, hint of destination.
With erasure, I could forget.

Daily, and without explanation,
more thread, the indescribable need to have things just so,
what to do after this thought ends.

From the doorjamb, a draft. The kickplate
sunken on one end. In pots on the step: geranium,
begonia, holes in their delicate fabric.

Gesture

Sometimes it is easiest to laugh
when I see myself in the mirror: the gray under my eyes
shades of purple really.

I am not so different that what happens to me
happens to me alone. Why am I showering
so early? Nothing could be more ridiculous.

I'm paid not to be late, and now
I am, having thought about you, me,
the good misery you say is yours.

Even in pain there is respite, in repetition
hallucination, a way of breaking through to
something else.

You break through, and I cannot help.
Only offer my hands.